5/24

W9-BMB-965

Judy Blume

My Favorite Writer

Jennifer Nault

WEIGL PUBLISHERS INC.

Published by Weigl Publishers Inc.
350 5th Avenue, Suite 3304
New York, NY 10118-0069
USA
Web site: www.weigl.com

Library of Congress Cataloging-in-Publication Data

Nault, Jennifer.
  Judy Blume / Jennifer Nault.
      p. cm. -- (My favorite writer)
Includes index.
Summary: A biography of American author Judy Blume, whose award-
winning children's books include "Are You There God? It's Me, Margaret"
and "Freckle Juice," plus a chapter of creative writing tips.
  ISBN 1-59036-025-7 (alk. paper)
 1. Blume, Judy--Juvenile literature. 2. Novelists, American--20th
century--Biography--Juvenile literature. 3. Children's stories--
Authorship--Juvenile literature. [1. Blume, Judy. 2. Authors,
American. 3. Women--Biography. 4. Authorship.] I. Title. II. Series.
  PS3552.L843 Z78 2002
  813'.54--dc21

                                             200200558

Editor
Jennifer Nault

Copy Editor
Heather Kissock

Design and Layout
Terry Paulhus

Photo Researcher
Tina Schwartzenberger

Printed in the United States
3 4 5 6 7 8 9 10 06 05

Contents

Milestones 5

Early Childhood 6

Growing Up 8

Learning the Craft 12

Getting Published 14

Writer Today 16

Popular Books 18

Creative Writing Tips 22

Writing a Biography Review . . . 24

Fan Information 26

Quiz 28

Writing Terms 30

Glossary 31

Index / Photo Credits 32

Judy Blume

MILESTONES

1938 Born on February 12 in Elizabeth, New Jersey

1961 Graduates from New York University with a degree in elementary education

1967 Takes a course on writing for children and teenagers at New York University

1970 *Are You There God? It's Me Margaret.* is published

1975 Divorces John Blume after sixteen years of marriage

1981 Establishes the Kids Fund to assist non-profit organizations that help young people

1996 Receives the Margaret Edwards Award

1998 *Summer Sisters* is published

Have you ever met someone who knows what you are thinking before you even say it? For many young readers, Judy Blume is that person. Fans of Judy Blume think of her as more than just their favorite author; she is a friend. Judy has been writing children's books for more than thirty years. One of her best-selling novels for young people is called *Are You There God? It's Me, Margaret.* It is the story of a girl and her experience of growing up. Often, the characters in Judy Blume's books are based on "regular" young people, just like her readers. Many children **identify** with the characters in Judy Blume's books. Judy has always tried to write the stories she wanted to read as a child.

Judy Blume's life has been filled with many accomplishments. Judy has written more than twenty-two books, which have been translated into twenty-six different languages. She is one of the best-loved children's writers of all time.

Early Childhood

Judy Blume was born Judy Sussman on February 12, 1938. She grew up in the city of Elizabeth, New Jersey. Judy's father, Rudolph, was a dentist. Esther, her mother, took care of Judy and her older brother, David.

Although Judy was a shy child, she had an active imagination. She loved to play make-believe games with her friends. When Judy played with her dolls, she would make up stories and stage plays. While she was a happy child, she had some fears, too. Judy was frightened of dogs, thunderstorms, and the dark.

The world was at war in the early 1940s. While Judy lived in the safety of her home in Elizabeth, World War II was being fought in Europe. Judy and her family would sit together and listen to news reports about the war on the radio. Sometimes, the news frightened her. Other times, Judy would dream about being a war hero.

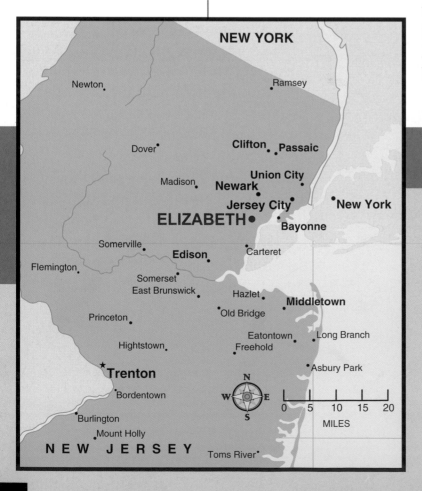

Judy Blume's birthplace, Elizabeth, was the first capital city of the state of New Jersey. Today, New Jersey's capital city is Trenton.

When the war ended in 1945, Judy was 7 years old. Today, Judy can still remember the day her family heard that the war was over. She was sitting with her mother and her grandmother, listening to the radio. A special announcement informed listeners that the war had ended. Her family jumped from their seats and started dancing around the room. Judy Blume's book *Starring Sally J. Freedman as Herself* is based on this period in her childhood. Sally, the book's main character, experiences a similar event when news breaks that the war is over.

After the war, life returned to normal. Judy loved going to school, and she especially loved reading books. Luckily, Judy did not have to look very far to find books. Her house was filled with them. Judy's mother was a keen reader, and her father was a book collector. Her favorite aunt, Frances, owned even more books. Judy would often visit her aunt to admire her large collection of books.

■ The Sussman family, along with people all over the United States, celebrated the end of World War II. In many places, people rejoiced in the streets.

Growing Up

Judy could not find any books about the experience of growing up that were written from a child's point of view.

Along with her fondness of reading, Judy also enjoyed writing. She liked class writing assignments, such as book reports. Sometimes, Judy would base her book reports on stories that she made up in her head. Fortunately, teachers never noticed. In fact, Judy often received excellent grades for her invented book reports.

When she was not in school or with friends, Judy's imagination kept her from boredom. Judy's stories were like good friends. They kept her company.

Judy's imagination could not shelter her from some sad experiences. By the time she was 10 years of age, a grandfather, a grandmother, an uncle, and an aunt had died. The loss of these loved ones made Judy think about the meaning of life. At the same time, Judy began to wonder what it was like to be an adult. Judy looked to books for the answers to these big questions, but came away disappointed. Judy could not find any books about the experience of growing up that were written from a child's point of view.

Meanwhile, Judy's brother, David, became sick. The Sussman's doctor told the family that moving to a warmer location would speed up his recovery. Miami Beach, Florida would be a fun getaway for the Sussman family—except for Judy's father. He had to stay in New Jersey to work at his dental practice. Judy knew that she would miss her father terribly.

Today, Judy Blume views the two years that she spent in Miami Beach as the most memorable years of her childhood. When the Sussmans first arrived, Judy was a little fearful about meeting people at a new school. However, she soon began to make friends. Over time, Judy's fears were replaced by a feeling of freedom. In Miami Beach, Judy had more freedom than she had ever known. Her time was spent going to school, playing outside, and heading to the beach on the weekends. The move to Miami Beach taught her an important life lesson: change can be good.

Inspired to Write

As a child, Judy Blume had an active imagination. She would make up stories and characters in her head. This tendency served Judy later in life when she decided to become a writer. Today, Judy's characters still live in her head. When she is occupied with a new book, the characters in her mind seem so real that she talks aloud to them.

Along with its sandy beaches, Judy enjoyed the sub-tropical climate of Miami Beach, Florida.

When the Sussmans returned to New Jersey, they came home to a surprise. Judy's father had bought the family a second-hand piano. Judy quickly signed up for piano lessons. She was disappointed to find out that learning to play the piano took a great deal of practice. Determined not to give up, Judy practiced regularly. Much later, Judy was to discover that writing was similar to learning to play the piano—practice makes perfect.

Judy became more outgoing after living in Miami Beach. In New Jersey, Judy attended Battin High School, an all-girl school. She and her friends joined several school clubs. Judy wrote for the school newspaper, performed with a dance group, and acted in school plays. Judy was a good student. She respected the teachers who encouraged students to think for themselves.

When she was practicing the piano, Judy would often pretend that she was giving piano lessons to her dolls.

Judy's circle of friends grew, as did her interests. Still, growing up was sometimes a confusing and lonely experience for Judy. She realized that the most difficult part of growing up was dealing with so many new feelings. Judy wondered if her peers felt the same way.

Although there were times when Judy felt alone, she also had many good friends. Her best friend was Mary Sullivan. While they shared many interests, their greatest interest was the theater. Sometimes, they attended plays in New York together. In the tenth grade, Judy and Mary decided to try out for parts in a school play. Fortunately, both of them were cast in the play. Judy was certain that she would become a well-known actress someday.

On their graduation day, Judy and Mary sat beside each other in their caps and gowns. While Judy had been a good student, she had learned much more than just math and spelling. She had tried many new things, such as acting, dancing, and writing for the school paper.

Judy Blume graduated from Battin High School with honors.

Favorite Authors

Judy's love of books began at an early age. When she was very young, her favorite book was *Madeline*, written by Ludwig Bemelmans. This book was about a little girl growing up in a French boarding school. Madeline's curiosity was always getting her into sticky situations. Judy loved this book so much that she hid it in a secret drawer. She believed that her copy from the public library was the only book in existence. Later, Judy began reading other books. She used her allowance to buy a Nancy Drew mystery each week. The Nancy Drew mystery series is written by Carolyn Keene. Judy also loved Betsy-Tacy books, written by Maud Hart Lovelace.

Learning the Craft

Although she had planned to teach Grade 2, Judy never worked as a teacher. Instead, she became a wife and mother.

When Judy was a child, she dreamed that her life would be filled with adventure. Growing up, her vision for the future changed many times. From spy, to ballerina, to pianist, to actress, Judy had many different **aspirations**. Still, she never gave any thought to becoming a writer.

After graduating high school, Judy went to New York University. She studied to become an elementary school teacher. While at university, Judy met and married John Blume. Although she had planned to teach Grade 2, Judy never worked as a teacher. Instead, she became a wife and mother.

Judy had always wanted children. By the time she was 25 years old, she had two. Judy had a daughter named Randy and a son named Larry. The Blumes lived in New Jersey. Judy enjoyed married life and loved her children. However, she felt that something was missing in her life. Judy, who still had an active imagination, needed to do something creative.

Judy studied ballet for many of her childhood years. She dreamed of becoming a well-known ballerina.

Judy pursued a career in songwriting. She quickly became discouraged because she felt that her songs lacked originality. Looking back on her life today, Judy Blume says that she never really decided to become a writer. It happened by accident. While doing household chores, Judy made up rhyming stories. She realized that she still enjoyed storytelling. Judy began to write and illustrate picture books for her own children.

One day, Judy received a pamphlet advertising a course in children's writing. Judy decided to take the course. The instructor, Lee Wyndham, was impressed with Judy's work. She felt that Judy was very talented and encouraged her to become a children's writer. Editors and publishers were invited to speak to the class. They inspired Judy to give writing a try. Judy enjoyed the course so much that she took it twice.

Inspired to Write

Judy Blume loves to stay active through exercise. She walks, bikes, or works out at the gym almost every day. Judy also likes to kayak. She gets some of her best story ideas when she is paddling out on the water. Along with keeping her healthy, exercise has another positive effect on Judy. It provides her with creative inspiration.

Many of Judy's books are set in the state of New Jersey, where the author was born and raised.

Getting Published

"I don't think anything
is as exciting as that
first acceptance."
Judy Blume

Judy Blume's first attempts at writing were picture books that she illustrated on her own with pencil crayons. With her writing improving every day, Judy decided it was time to send her stories to publishers. Her writing instructor and classmates supported Judy's decision.

Judy's heart fell when she opened her first response letter from a publisher. Her book had been rejected. At first, Judy felt like a failure—she was used to succeeding in her efforts. After a while, Judy learned to handle publishers' rejection letters. She believed in herself and was determined to become a writer.

Finally, after two years of rejection slips, magazines began publishing Judy's short stories. Her first book was published in 1969. A publishing company accepted Judy's picture book called *The One in the Middle is the Green Kangaroo*. While Judy was not paid very much, that did not matter—she was finally a published author.

The Publishing Process

Publishing companies receive hundreds of **manuscripts** from authors each year. Only a few manuscripts become books. Publishers must be sure that a manuscript will sell many copies. As a result, publishers reject most of the manuscripts they receive.

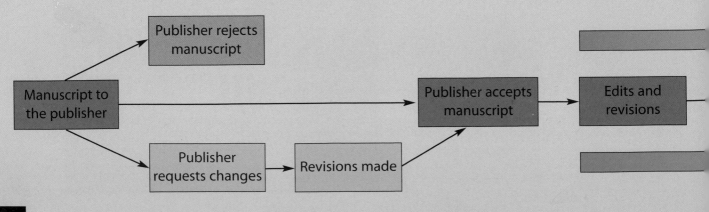

Judy's next book was a novel for young readers called *Iggie's House*. It went through several stages before it was published. A publishing company called Bradbury Press told Judy that they were interested in the book. They also told her that she would have to make **revisions** before they would publish it. She worked on the story with Dick Jackson, an editor, and it was finally accepted. Judy was on a roll.

She soon discovered a new hurdle in the world of publishing—**reviewers**. Some reviewers disliked Judy's book. The new author learned that she would not be able to please everyone with her writing. By the time *Iggie's House* was on shelves, Judy had already begun writing another book. It was called *Are You There God? It's Me, Margaret*. Judy had no idea that this book would become a bestseller. It changed her life, along with children's publishing, forever.

Inspired to Write

Many of Judy Blume's children's books have similar **themes**. Some of the themes are based on Judy's own childhood and life experiences. Themes central to Judy's writing include: growing up, relationships, fitting in, facing fears, determination, and loneliness. No matter how serious the topic, Judy always looks for humor in the situation.

Once a manuscript has been accepted, it goes through many stages before it is published. Often, authors change their work to follow an editor's suggestions. Once the book is published, some authors receive royalties. This is money based on book sales.

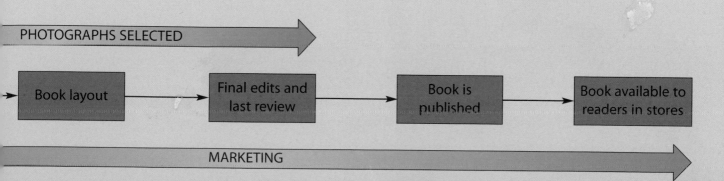

PHOTOGRAPHS SELECTED →

Book layout → Final edits and last review → Book is published → Book available to readers in stores

MARKETING →

Writer Today

oday, Judy Blume is more than 60 years of age. She is still very active and youthful. Writing has remained an important part of Judy's life. She writes almost every day to get her ideas down on paper.

In 1975, Judy's marriage to John Blume ended in divorce. In 1987, she married a writer of **nonfiction**, George Cooper. Her children are now adults, and Judy has been blessed with a grandson, Elliot. It should not be surprising that Elliot's first word was "book." Randy, his mother, has followed in her mother's footsteps. She recently wrote a book called *Crazy in the Cockpit*. Randy dedicated the book to her mother.

Over the years, Judy has lived in different parts of the United States. When her children finished elementary school, Judy and her family moved to New Mexico. They lived there for seven years. For a short period after that, Judy lived in Connecticut. Today, Judy still has trouble staying in one place. She has homes in New York City, New York; Key West, Florida; and on the island of Martha's Vineyard off the coast of Massachusetts.

■ More than 75 million copies of Judy's books have been sold worldwide.

In 1999, Judy Blume came out with a new novel for adults called *Summer Sisters*. It jumped to the top of the New York Times bestseller list. After writing that novel, she went back to children's writing with another book in her Fudge series of books. It is called *Double Fudge*. She dedicated it to her grandson, Elliot, who is one of Fudge's greatest fans. To her readers' delight, Judy says that she is not finished writing books. She still has too many stories to tell.

Judy still loves writing. Writing allows her to play make-believe, like she did as a child. Even when life has been difficult, Judy has continued to write. According to Judy, writing keeps her feeling young by allowing her to feel "forever 12 years old."

Judy Blume writes books about sensitive childhood issues. Many of her stories seem as though they are taken directly from a young person's diary.

Popular Books

Author Judy Blume is best known for her books for children and teenagers. Judy also writes novels for adults. Many of the people who read Judy Blume's adult **fiction** grew up reading her children's books. Following are some of Judy's best-loved children's books:

Are You There God? It's Me, Margaret.

Children have adored the tale of Margaret Simon since it was first published. The central character, Margaret, wants to grow up too fast. While she is only 11 years old, she cannot wait to become an adult. In the beginning of the book, Margaret's family moves to New Jersey. She has to adjust to a new way of life and a new school. Margaret makes friends with some girls at school. They decide to have a competition to see which of them begins to show signs of growing up first. Margaret has many questions about reaching **maturity**, but she does not feel comfortable sharing her concerns with others. This leaves Margaret with many unanswered questions. She is excited to be entering the world of **adolescence**, yet she is also scared. Margaret's loneliness is eased when she begins to share her feelings with God.

AWARDS
Are You There God? It's Me, Margaret.

1970 Outstanding Book of the Year, New York Times

1975 Nene Award

1976 Young Hoosier Award, Indiana Media Educators

1979 North Dakota Children's Choice Book Award

1980 Great Stone Face Award, New Hampshire Library Association

JUDY BLUME

Are You There God? It's Me, Margaret.

Tales of a Fourth Grade Nothing

As if going through the fourth grade was not enough of a challenge! *Tales of a Fourth Grade Nothing* is one of Judy Blume's five Fudge books. The book tells the story of Peter Hatcher; his little brother, Fudge; his baby sister, Tootsie; and their neighbor, Sheila Tubman. Peter is the oldest child. He must constantly deal with little Fudge's antics and meddling. Fudge is impossible, and Peter's parents are no better. They think that Fudge is perfect. Peter's parents do not believe that Fudge gives his older brother so much trouble. This means that Peter is often left to look out for himself. *Tales of a Fourth Grade Nothing* is a humorous book with many silly episodes. The wacky antics of the Hatcher brothers and their neighbors will make readers laugh out loud.

Freckle Juice

Freckle Juice is a humorous book about a young boy named Andrew. More than anything in the world, Andrew wants to have freckles. His school friend, Nicky, has freckles that cover his face, ears, and neck. Andrew asks Nicky how to get freckles. A classmate offers to sell Andrew a special potion that will give him freckles. Andrew accepts the offer. When he brews up the freckle juice, he is more than surprised at the results.

AWARDS
Tales of a Fourth Grade Nothing
1980 West Australian Young Reader's Book Award
1981 Great Stone Face Award, New Hampshire Library Council
1983 Massachusetts Children's Book Award

AWARDS
Freckle Juice
1980 Michigan Young Reader's Award

Starring Sally J. Freedman as Herself

This book is the most **autobiographical** of all of Judy Blume's books. In *Starring Sally J. Freedman as Herself*, Sally is full of fantastic ideas. It is 1947, and 10-year-old Sally moves with her family to Miami Beach so that her brother can recover from a serious illness. The sad thing is that Sally's father has to stay behind. Sally also has to make new friends at school. She tries to convince her new friends that she is more grown-up and worldly than she really feels. Sally's school year away from home is an exciting read.

AWARDS
Blubber

1974 Outstanding Book of the Year, *New York Times*
1983 North Dakota Children's Choice Award

Blubber

Although *Blubber* begins as a funny tale, it deals with some troubling issues, such as bullying in the classroom. Jill is a typical young girl—she likes to read and to collect stamps. She also likes having friends. To stay popular, Jill joins the rest of the fifth-grade class taunting Linda, a classmate who is overweight. Although Jill feels uncomfortable with her classmates' actions, she does little to stop it. On Halloween, Jill learns a big lesson when she becomes the new target of the students' torments.

Here's to You, Rachel Robinson

Rachel is a straight-A student who feels pressured at home and at school. She just wants to be a normal kid, but teachers keep trying to put her in **accelerated** school programs. Rachel's family life is also complicated. Her brother is thrown out of boarding school and sent home. He is disruptive and taunts his family constantly, but Rachel's friends find him charming. People are putting more and more pressure on Rachel. She is expected to become class president, play the flute, volunteer as a peer counselor, and take a leading role in the school play all at once. How will Rachel deal with the pressure?

Otherwise Known as Sheila the Great

Otherwise Known as Sheila the Great is another of Judy Blume's Fudge books. The main character is Sheila Tubman, Peter Hatcher's neighbor. Sheila Tubman sometimes feels as though she is two different people. On the outside she is "Sheila the Great"—outgoing, witty, and brave. On the inside, she feels less brave. Sheila is afraid of dogs, spiders, swimming, and the dark. Sheila's family decides to spend the summer in Tarrytown, New York. This means that she finally has to face some of her worst fears: Sheila has a close encounter with a dog, and her parents expect her to take swimming lessons. How will Sheila stay afloat?

Iggie's House

In Judy's second book, an African-American family moves into an all-white neighborhood. The main character, Winnie, befriends her new neighbors, the Garbers. Many of the people living on Grove Street disapprove of Winnie's friendship with the Garbers. Unhappy with the behavior of her neighbors, Winnie is determined to fight for the acceptance of the Garber family.

AWARDS
Here's to You, Rachel Robinson
1993 Parents' Choice Award

AWARDS
Otherwise Known as Sheila the Great
1978 South Carolina Children's Book Award
1982 South Carolina Children's Book Award
1984 Book of the Month Award, German Academy for Children's and Young People's Literature

Creative Writing Tips

Writing a poem, a novel, or even a school report can be challenging. It is also very rewarding. The following writing tips will help keep you on track when you are writing:

Keep a Writing Journal

Most authors do not come up with a complete story all at once. They may come up with an idea for an interesting character or a funny **scene**. Make sure to record your ideas in a writing journal while they are still fresh in your mind. Judy Blume uses a journal to jot down her ideas while she is planning a new book. She may end up with pages and pages of scribbles about different characters.

Use Your Own Experiences

If you are stuck for a story idea, write about a subject that you know well—you! Some people think that their lives are not interesting enough for a story. Do not make that mistake. Touching or funny things have happened to everyone. For instance, what was your first day at school like? You can begin with the truth and then add details to make the story funny, sad, or silly.

■ Before she begins writing, Judy Blume jots down everything that comes into her head, including background details.

Do It Your Own Way

Aspiring writers will hear many differing opinions on the subject of writing. Some people say that it is best to write early in the morning. Others believe that writers are most creative when they work in the evening. Some authors need to listen to music, while others require complete silence. You have to discover your own comfort zone. Some authors come up with a detailed **outline** before they begin to write a story. Judy Blume does not write this way. She usually knows how the story begins, but she writes the rest as she goes.

Review and Revise

Very few great stories are completed in just one **draft**. Often, writers need to read their work with a **critical eye**. Revising is an important part of the writing process. Sometimes, a story needs a little extra attention to make it shine. Reading over your work several times is one way to improve the quality of your writing. Judy Blume revises by reading her story aloud. When you hear your story out loud, it becomes easier to decide where improvements can be made. This part of the writing process is Judy's favorite. She will often revise a story three or four times before she feels that it is ready for publication.

Inspired to Write

Judy Blume is an active member of several organizations related to her life's work. She is a member of the Author's Guild and the Society of Children's Book Writers and Illustrators. She is also the founder of a organization called the Kids Fund. It is a charitable and educational foundation that funds educational and writing opportunities for children.

Today, Judy likes to write in a small cabin on the island of Martha's Vineyard.

Writing a Biography Review

A biography is an account of an individual's life that is written by another person. Some people's lives are very interesting. In school, you may be asked to write a biography review. The first thing to do when writing a biography review is to decide whom you would like to learn about. Your school library or community library will have a large selection of biographies from which to choose.

Are you interested in an author, a sports figure, an inventor, a movie star, or a president? Finding the right book is your first task. Whether you choose to write your review on a biography of Judy Blume or another person, the task will be similar.

Begin your review by writing the title of the book, the author, and the person featured in the book. Then, start writing about the main events in the person's life. Include such things as where the person grew up and what his or her childhood was like. You will want to add details about the person's adult life, such as whether he or she married or had children. Next, write about what you think makes this person special. What kinds of experiences influenced this individual? For instance, did he or she grow up in unusual circumstances? Was the person determined to accomplish a goal? Include any details that surprised you. A concept web is a useful research tool. Use the concept web on the right to begin researching your biography review.

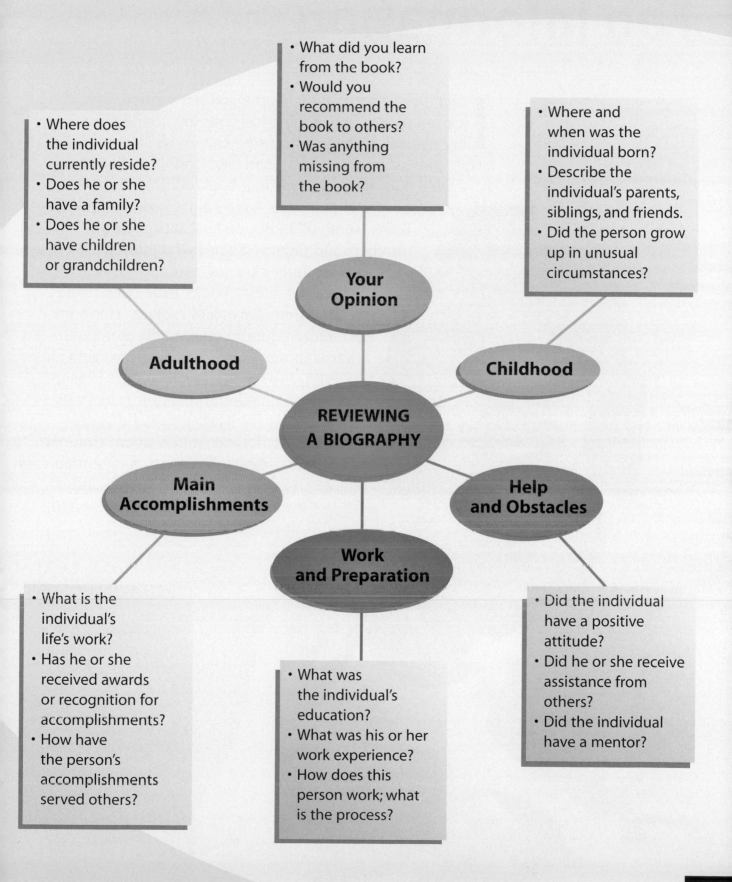

- Where does the individual currently reside?
- Does he or she have a family?
- Does he or she have children or grandchildren?

- What did you learn from the book?
- Would you recommend the book to others?
- Was anything missing from the book?

- Where and when was the individual born?
- Describe the individual's parents, siblings, and friends.
- Did the person grow up in unusual circumstances?

Your Opinion

Adulthood

Childhood

REVIEWING A BIOGRAPHY

Main Accomplishments

Help and Obstacles

Work and Preparation

- What is the individual's life's work?
- Has he or she received awards or recognition for accomplishments?
- How have the person's accomplishments served others?

- What was the individual's education?
- What was his or her work experience?
- How does this person work; what is the process?

- Did the individual have a positive attitude?
- Did he or she receive assistance from others?
- Did the individual have a mentor?

Fan Information

If you are a fan of Judy Blume and her writing, you are not alone. Judy Blume has a strong connection to her readers. During her writing career, she has received a tremendous amount of fan mail. Judy published some of the letters from her fans in a book entitled, *Letters to Judy: What Your Kids Wish They Could Tell You.* Today, some of Judy's earliest fans are now mothers and fathers. Their own children are reading Judy's stories, too.

Many of Judy's books have been made into television shows and movies. Her books have received more than ninety different awards in the United States and worldwide. In 1983, Judy Blume received the Eleanor Roosevelt Humanitarian Award. In 1996, she received the Margaret A. Edwards Award for Lifetime Achievement from the American Library Association. Children's Choice Awards are very special to Judy because those awards are selected by children.

Judy Blume believes that parents should communicate openly with their children. Young people need someone to turn to when they feel lonely, sad, or confused.

Judy thinks that it is very important to keep in touch with her fans, so she has a special Web site for them. Now, along with answering letters, Judy is busy answering e-mails sent to her Web site, too. She loses track of time when she is responding to e-mails. Just as her readers get caught up in her books, Judy gets caught up in her fans' lives.

Author

Judy Blume

When I was growing up, I dreamed about becoming a cowgirl, a detective, a spy, a great actress, or a ballerina. Not a dentist, like my father, or a homemaker, like my mother -- and certainly not a writer, although I always loved to read. I didn't know anything about writers. It never occurred to me they were regular people and that I could grow up to become one, even though I loved to make up stories inside my head.

WEB LINKS

Kid's Reads

www.kidsreads.com/authors/au-blume-judy.asp

This Web site provides visitors with a great biography of Judy Blume. They can explore this Web site to find out about other children's authors from the United States.

Judy Blume's Home Base

www.judyblume.com

Judy Blume's Web site is packed with so much information that her fans will be entertained for hours. Visitors to the site can look at photographs and read Judy's writing tips.

Quiz

Q: Where and when was Judy Blume born?

1

A: Judy Blume was born in Elizabeth, New Jersey on February 12, 1938.

2

Q: Where did Judy Blume spend two years of her childhood?

A: Miami Beach, Florida

3

Q: What instrument did Judy Blume's father buy for his family?

A: A piano

4

Q: Who was Judy's best friend in high school?

A: Mary Sullivan

5

Q: Judy studied to become an elementary school teacher. Did she ever work as a teacher?

A: No, she raised a family instead

6

Q: What are the names of Judy's two children?

A: Randy and Larry

Q: Where does Judy Blume currently reside?

A: Judy has homes in New York City, New York; Key West, Florida; and on the island of Martha's Vineyard in Massachusetts.

8

Q: Judy recently wrote a book called *Double Fudge* as part of her Fudge series of books. To whom did she dedicate it?

A: Judy dedicated the book to her grandson, Elliot.

9

Q: What is Judy's favorite part of the writing process?

A: Revising her writing

10

Q: How many different awards has Judy won for her writing over the years?

A: Judy has won more than ninety awards.

Writing Terms

This glossary will introduce you to some of the main terms in the field of writing. Understanding these common writing terms will allow you to discuss your ideas about books and writing with others.

action: the moving events of a work of fiction

antagonist: the person in the story who opposes the main character

autobiography: a history of a person's life written by that person

biography: a written account of another person's life

character: a person in a story, poem, or play

climax: the most exciting moment or turning point in a story

episode: a short piece of action, or scene, in a story

fiction: stories about characters and events that are not real

foreshadow: hinting at something that is going to happen later in the book

imagery: a written description of a thing or idea that brings an image to mind

narrator: the speaker of the story who relates the events

nonfiction: writing that deals with real people and events

novel: published writing of considerable length that portrays characters within a story

plot: the order of events in a work of fiction

protagonist: the leading character of a story; often a likable character

resolution: the end of the story, when the conflict is settled

scene: a single episode in a story

setting: the place and time in which a work of fiction occurs

theme: an idea that runs throughout a work of fiction

Glossary

accelerated: caused faster progress

adolescence: the time between puberty and adulthood

aspirations: strong desires and hopes

aspiring: working toward a goal

autobiographical: written account of one's own life

critical eye: having the ability to judge something fairly

draft: a rough copy of something written

fiction: stories about characters and events that are not real

identify: to connect with an audience

manuscripts: drafts of stories before they are published

maturity: the state of being fully developed, or grown up

nonfiction: writing that deals with real people and events

outline: the framework of a story

reviewers: people whose job it is to say or write their opinions

revisions: alterations to a manuscript in order to correct or improve it

scene: a single episode in a story

themes: central ideas that run throughout works of fiction

Index

Are You There God? It's Me, Margaret. 5, 15, 18

Battin High School 10, 11
Bemelmans, Ludwig 11
Blume, John 5, 12, 16
Bradbury Press 15

Cooper, George 16

Double Fudge 17, 29

Elizabeth, New Jersey 5, 6, 28

Here's to You, Rachel Robinson 21

Iggie's House 15, 21

Jackson, Dick 15

Keene, Carolyn 11
Kids Fund 5, 23

Lovelace, Maud Hart 11

Martha's Vineyard, Massachusetts 16, 23, 29
Miami Beach, Florida 9, 10, 20, 28

New York University 5, 12

One in the Middle is the Green Kangaroo, The 14
Otherwise Known as Sheila the Great 21

Starring Sally J. Freedman as Herself 7, 20
Sullivan, Mary 11, 29
Summer Sisters 5, 17

Tales of a Fourth Grade Nothing 19

World War II 6, 7
Wyndham, Lee 13

Photo Credits

Cover illustration by Terry Paulhus
AP Photo/Suzanne Plunkett: page 4; Courtesy of Bantam Doubleday
Dell Books for Young Readers: pages 18, 19, 20; Scott Barrow: page 13;
©Bettmann/CORBIS/MAGMA: pages 1, 3, 16, 26; EyeWire, Inc.: pages 10, 17, 22;
Eric Kamp/MaXx Images: page 23; Courtesy of www.kidsreads.com: page 27;
Map Resources: page 6; New York Times Co./Archive Photos: page 7; PhotoDisc:
pages 12, 28; PhotoSpin, Inc.: page 11; Scott Smith/MaXx Images: pages 8–9.